CHOOSE
JOY

CHOOSE JOY

BRIDGING THE GAP BETWEEN GOD'S GLORY
AND OUR GREATEST GOOD

CAMERON ROY

LUCIDBOOKS

Choose Joy
Copyright © 2016 by Cameron Roy

Published by Lucid Books in Houston, TX.
www.LucidBooks.net

First Printing 2016

ISBN 10: 1-63296-084-2
ISBN 13: 978-1-63296-084-9
eISBN 10: 1-63296-085-0
eISBN 13: 978-1-63296-085-6

Special Sales: Most Lucid Books titles are available in special quantity discounts. Custom imprinting or excerpting can also be done to fit special needs. Contact Lucid Books at info@lucidbooks.net.

This book is dedicated
to all the people
who helped me
to see, understand, believe,
and fall in love
with this beautiful truth.

TABLE OF CONTENTS

ACKNOWLEDGMENTS

Credit needs to be given where credit is due. This book would not have been possible without a number of people in my life directly and indirectly.

The first people I need to thank are my parents. My mother has always been my biggest fan and knows how to bring out the best in me and because of her I know what hard and diligent work looks like and how big of an impact attitude has on the things we find ourselves doing in this life. My father has always supported anything and everything I've set my mind to do and, because of him, I know dreams and goals can be accomplished with dedication and perseverance. I'm forever indebted to both of them for their love, compassion, patience, and inspiration they have given to me in my 23 years of life.

Everything I've written about in this book was learned from listening to, reading from, and studying with brilliant people who love the Lord and have dedicated their lives to helping people see that Christ is the reward. Those who directly influenced me are, but not limited to, Dusty Thompson, Rashard Barnes, Dick Courtney, Kyle Struzyk, Matthew Gill, Coleman Maxwell, Mitchell Johnson, Tanner Dean, Jackson Bailey, Ben Cooper, Jack Cassels, Banner Owen, Campbell Roper, the men associated with Men of God Christian Fraternity Inc. Those who indirectly influenced me are, but not limited to, John Piper, J.I. Packer, Matt Chandler, Eric Mason, David Platt, Todd Wagner, Jonathan Pokluda, Andy Stanley, Ben Stuart, Ravi Zacharias, Jonathan Edwards, C.S. Lewis, and Martin Luther.

SPECIAL THANKS

This book would be nothing more than a file saved on my computer had it not been for the very gracious people who helped finance this book. These people blew me away by their generosity when they didn't have to do anything. These amazing people are:

Chance & Kristi Payton
Clark & Cindy Roy
Neal & Joe Roy
Ben & Kaylee Cooper
Jackson & Sydney Cassels
Banner Owen
Shawn, Carrie & Brittany Spivey
Bryan Nowlin
Ron & Shelly Mann
Deanna Logan
Jerry & Denise Barnes
Kelton & Maecee Coleman
Sharon Griffith
Cindy Williams
Bill & Tracy Paulk
Sue Ann Ricketts
John & Debbie Cooper
Matthew & Sabrina Gill
Dale & Brooke Woodul
Mason Morrow

INTRODUCTION

I grew up in a small West Texas town. The kind of town where everyone knows everyone's business, what kind of trouble they may be in, the person they're dating, or the money they're making. In this kind of town, few people keep secrets.

Growing up there was a lot of fun. We had little to do, so my friends and I had to create our own fun. Sledding on car hoods behind trucks, mudding, toilet papering houses, setting fireworks off in the middle of town at midnight, and pranking people were activities we would often find ourselves doing.

Being from West Texas, I was raised in the general area of the Bible Belt. I was a small-town Baptist kid who was dragged to church every Sunday by his mom and sat on the front row pew with the youth. I volunteered heavily, sang hymns, and even went on every church camp or retreat available. Everyone saw me as a "good kid" because of my accomplishments in school, sports, and church involvement. When I wanted to have some good fun, I would usually just have to subdue my conscience for a night so I didn't feel guilty.

I thought I was doing well in my relationship with God. I figured I knew all I needed to know about God and His love for me. I could do what I wanted to do to be happy, and when

I asked for forgiveness, God would forgive me. What an amazing life to live, right?

I finished out my eighteen years in my hometown and headed for college, aiming to make it into the music industry. I had loved music my entire life, had secured an Associate degree in commercial music, and desired the life of a musician. But something inside of me was pressing into my soul that made me feel guilty for desiring that lifestyle. I did not want drugs, sex, and wealth; I just wanted to make a living doing what made me happy. Was that too much to ask for? The problem was that when I was sixteen, I had been called by the Lord into ministry at a camp called Super Summer in Abilene, Texas. One night during the worship session, I felt God calling me to His work. I have never been able to explain it, but I was confident in the call. I still wanted a life of music, so I just let ministry slowly fade out of my mind and filled it with the fantasy of a life in music.

I told some people about this conviction and guilt I had been feeling about wanting to pursue a life of music, and the majority of people that I told all communicated the same thought: "Cameron, it looks like God is calling you to trust and obey Him." I thought to myself, I have "obeyed" Him. I go to church. I'm involved in a Bible study. I've led events and volunteered in the church. I wondered, isn't that enough to make Him happy? Can't I also do something that will make me happy?

But in my sophomore year of college, God would begin calling me into a deeper relationship with Him. I began to meet people who confronted me with questions about God and His characteristics that made me uneasy. They refused to accept my surface answers and instead demanded that I speak honestly about where I was with God. These encounters would begin to change much of my understanding of God and would lead me on to change my thinking about how to live a truly joyful life.

Have you ever pondered why God would command us to obey Him? Why He would call us into areas where we have to make sacrifices in order to follow Him? I had to ask myself,

"If God is so good and loves me, then why wouldn't He be on board with what I love if I'm also serving Him? Why would He call me away from my passions?" There had to be more than just submissive obedience to His will for my life.

That is why I'm writing this book—to help give you the peace that our happiness and God's glory do not contradict one another. That His will for our lives is never about Him acting as a dictator commanding us to obey Him, but rather Him offering an invitation into the deepest joy we can experience this side of glory.

My aim and desire in this book is to help you become a joy seeker—to bridge the gap of God's glory and your joy in a completely biblical manner. The problem has never been God misunderstanding what would make us most happy in this life; the problem is that we have not understood what would make us most happy in this life. God is not looking to bind us. He is setting us free.

THE PURSUIT OF JOY

J ust by observing human behavior, we can likely agree we were made for happiness, pleasure, and joy. Everything we do is rooted in a desire to be happy. The famous mathematician, Blaise Pascal, explains it perfectly: "All men seek happiness. This is without exception. Whatever different means they employ, they all tend to this end. The cause of some going to war, and of others avoiding it, is the same desire in both, attended with different views. The will never takes the least step but to this object. This is the motive of every action of every man, even of those who hang themselves."[1]

We often pursue what we *believe* will make us happy, which can be different from what will truly bring us joy and is for our good. For example, consider the man who hangs himself. He hangs himself because he is tired of all the unhappiness. He simply wants the unhappiness to end, even if it means hanging

---

1. Blaise Pascal, *Pensees* (Mineola, NY: Dover Publications, 2003), 113, https://books.google.com/books?id=qpYwR3FT0-kC&printsec=frontcover&source=gbs_ge_summary_r&cad=0#v=onepage&q=All%20men%20seek%20happiness.%20&f=false.

himself to do it. While this act will end his pain, however, it is not what is best for him.

When I reflect on my childhood and the advice from teachers, family, friends, famous people, the media, and anyone else, I was told to be happy. Maybe you can relate. When I started athletics in the seventh grade, I was 4'11" and weighed 92 pounds. I was the guy everyone wanted to face in tackling drills because I was so little. Most of my friends were getting into protein shakes, creatinine pills, and mass gainers, so I decided to join in. Why? Because those things would make me bigger, faster, and stronger. What would that make me? Happy.

Then, later on as I was deciding what to study in college, my grandmother wanted me to pursue accounting. Why? Because accounting meant a secure job, a secure job meant money, and what did money mean? Happiness.

Many women give their time and finances to look a certain way. They work out daily, follow a strict diet, buy the best makeup, and create an unhealthy relationship with their mirror as they examine every square inch of their body. Why? Because if they look a certain way, they'll be approved by men and women, which will make them...you guessed it, happy.

We are active seekers of happiness in everything we do.

But our pursuit of happiness doesn't just affect the jobs we pursue, the clothes we buy, or the colleges we choose. It filters into our view of God. Many people pray because they want God to bring them happiness. They believe, without realizing it, that their enjoyment is in God because He gives them "stuff." A common theme running throughout today's culture is that our greatest good is whatever we want it to be. For example, a musician's greatest good might be to reach the top of the billboards, or an actor's greatest good could be to win an Oscar. If we desire something, it must be good for us. When pursuing a personal goal or ambition, many Christians, including myself, turn to Philippians 4:13: "I can do all things through him who strengthens me." We decide what we are going to do, when we are going to do it, and how we are going do it, and then bring God in and ask Him to take care of it. We essentially bring God into our own agenda instead of considering what God would want us to do.

Psalm 37:4 is another popular verse among Christians: "Delight yourself in the LORD, and he will give you the desires of your heart." Some people read that verse and think, "All the desires of my heart will be given to me, if I just delight myself in God? I'll take that God." These people unknowingly end up treating God like Santa Claus. The teaching of Santa is that if you don't believe, you don't receive. Kids believe if they're good and treat Santa like royalty by decorating the house, baking cookies for him, and welcoming him cheerfully, come Christmastime, he'll give them what they asked for.

But what if Christmas arrived and Santa brought only himself, instead of the things the child asked for? Would the child be happy, or disappointed? Think about God in this way. Why do you like God? Are you happy with just God Himself, regardless of whether He gives you the things you ask for?

The Definitions of Happiness and Joy

Many misconceptions exist as to what the words *happiness* and *joy* mean. I have heard people use both happiness and joy in the same sentence when those words were both irrelevant to the situation being discussed. If we're going to be a people chasing after joy, we have to gain clarity on what happiness means and what joy means, because what we pursue to make us happy stems from our definitions of happiness and joy. The challenge is that we are immersed in western culture, and we often use that culture to determine what we do and do not believe about joy and happiness. Thankfully, however, the Bible lays out situations where both of these words are used so that we can understand a biblical definition.

Happiness

In Genesis, the Bible tells the story of Rachel and Leah's dispute involving their husband, Jacob. Both Rachel and Leah wanted to please Jacob by giving birth to male children. Eventually, Rachel found out she could not get pregnant, so she offered her servant Bilhah to Jacob to conceive a son. This practice of offering servants to husbands was part of Ancient Near-Eastern culture, and the resulting child was considered to be the wife's regardless of the servant being the one who gave birth to the child. Bilhah did conceive two sons with Jacob, Dan and Naphtali, whom Rachel named.

After having four sons, Leah discovered she also was barren, so she offered her servant Zilpah to Jacob in order to conceive a son. Zilpah conceived two sons with Jacob, Gad and Asher, whom Leah named. When Zilpah had given birth, Leah said, "Happy am I! For women have called me happy" (Gen. 30:13). Now, in the context of this story, Leah stated she was "happy" because what she had wanted finally happened. After her servant bore sons, Leah used this word "happy," showing that the words happy or happiness relate to circumstances turning out the way someone desires them to.

The Cool Kids

When I was in elementary school, the place to shop for clothes was Abercrombie. I went there because all of my friends did and wearing Abercrombie's clothes was a platform for popularity. We all bought into the look and status Abercrombie could give us. When I entered into middle school, however, American Eagle became the place to shop. The clothes were no different except for the logos: a bird versus a moose.

So why did I change? Why did I sell out from Abercrombie and move my spending to American Eagle? Because of the promise that American Eagle would bring me popularity and approval, and approval would make me...happy. But that was the exact same promise Abercrombie had given me, so why did I switch? Because everyone else I knew had changed, and therefore what was once acceptable, satisfying, and gave me a sense of belonging no longer brought those things. The same clothing that was once cool became "un-cool" because other people said it was uncool.

But this false sense of happiness doesn't happen just with teen clothing. I find it ironic that every advertisement also promises some sense of happiness in whatever it's selling. Consider the iPhone, for example. Apple has released multiple iPhone versions over the years, and I do not recall any commercial or advertisement for the iPhone ever saying, "This one will hold you over and satisfy you until the next model comes out." Instead, every product is marketed to communicate, "This is it! This will satisfy your deepest pleasure and desire for happiness. You need this!"

But then what happens? More technology comes out, or a new fashion style, so that the great "thing" is no longer satisfying because it's not "in." We then need something else to be satisfied—the newest version, the updated software, that new car, a new look.

The world tells us the means for satisfaction is keeping up with the world, its things, and doing whatever culture approves at that time. According to our culture, in order to be satisfied we have to keep up, but often keeping up means we throw out something old we once thought would make us happy. It is ironic, though, that what we have to give up was at one time the "new" thing we bought into, the same thing that told us, 'this will make us someone'. If you want to continue to be happy, you'll have to toss your old possession aside and buy into what is new.

Happiness, then, is based on circumstances. Its definition changes between culture and decades and depends on what people tell us will make us satisfied. Happiness will change, depending on our surroundings.

Joy

How does joy differ from happiness? Does the difference even matter? As we begin to think about the true meaning of joy, let's look at the book of James. James was the brother of Jesus and used the word *joy* in a context that might just surprise you.

James 1:2

"Count it all joy, my brothers, when you meet trials of various kinds."

Isn't it odd that James would instruct us to find joy in trials? Why would a difficult chapter in our lives be considered a source of joy? James answers that for us in the next verses.

James 1:3-4

"For you know that the testing of your faith produces steadfastness. And let steadfastness have its full effect, that you may be perfect and complete, lacking in nothing."

The text in James is clear: the testing of our faith develops steadfastness, refining us into more perfect and complete followers of Christ, people who joyfully submit to His authority and will for our lives. Knowing that we are being made steadfast in the faith doesn't mean that we are becoming people who won't be affected by trials, but that we are becoming more committed to Christ no matter the cost. This is a glorious truth if you believe that Christ is your reward. It seems as though joy has to do with knowledge and trust of something that isn't current, but surely coming according to the promises of God.

Joy is founded in the firm trust that God's promises are true in every circumstance.

We are a people looking for happiness and satisfaction, but we often look for happiness from every source except God. The problem is that we have not taken God at His word:

Psalm 16:11

"You make known to me the path of life; in your presence there is fullness of joy; at your right hand are pleasures forevermore."

You see, God promises that walking with Him will give us true joy and pleasure. Culture, however, tells us that it's not God, but possessions, status, money, jobs, and relationships that will bring "fullness of joy." But how many times have these things given us complete satisfaction or lasting happiness? Never! The marketing ads, if correctly put, should read, "This item is a temporary fulfillment of your deepest quest for pleasure, happiness, and joy. It will only last until the next big product comes out." Even though we often know deep down that these ads are not true, we still let society and its promises of happiness constantly compete with God's promises. Regardless, as we've already discussed, the only consistency we can count on from "things" is their inconsistency to satisfy us.

Isaiah 40:8

"The grass withers, the flower fades, but the word of our God will stand forever."

How amazing that statement is! The supercharged and explosively satisfying word of God will stand forever. But what is our typical pattern, even when God has promised us incredible truths? We keep turning to money, jobs, and relationships, believing that if we just get one more thing, we'll be happy. Yet, we're left feeling as if something is missing. This world and all of its pleasures seem as if they will last, but they have proven time and again that they are fleeting. Some people tell us that God's word is irrelevant in today's times and changes, that we need to get on board with these changes because they are right. But the longest period of time an iPhone stood is one year. Each year there has to be a newer look, a better color, and a new feature that makes taking a selfie easier. There is no satisfaction forever, only long enough for someone to create a newer, shinier promise.

The apostle Paul explains we were created for pleasure, but not in the way we typically think:

2 Corinthians 1:24

"Not that we lord it over your faith, but we work with you for your joy, for you stand firm in your faith."

Paul explains to the church in Corinth that one of his purposes in his ministry was that they would have joy, which would in turn fuel their faith in God. As 1 John 5:4 explains, "And this is the victory that has overcome the world—our faith." True faith means we are satisfied with all that God has given us in and through Jesus, and that satisfaction is the foundation for lasting, pure joy.

Paul knew better than anyone that the pursuit of pleasure could be completed only in Jesus. Savoring Jesus as the most satisfying being in the world will end the relentless and restless search for joy, because nothing can compete with the satisfaction He offers. There is no new fad, movement, person, technology or anything that could satisfy us more than the Triune God.

THE SOURCES OF TRUE JOY

A lthough we now have a working definition of true joy, we need to dig a little deeper to begin to understand how we can achieve joy. It's not enough to just understand what joy is—we also need to grasp where it comes from. Let's look more specifically at the true sources of joy.

True Joy Stems from Obedience

Consistent, lasting joy cannot exist apart from obeying God. Obedience is one of the core principles of living the Christian life. However, as we begin to grow in obedience to God, we also have to grow in our trust in Him. Obedience and trust must walk hand in hand. But how does increasing our trust in God lead to joy? Why would simple trust bring us satisfaction? Let's dive a little deeper into the ideas of trust and obedience.

When I was growing up, the person I listened to the most was my grandfather, whom I call Pops. I consider Pops my life mentor. When he told me no, I didn't fight back as much as I did with other people. At that age, I would argue with those who wanted to challenge my reasoning, and I would question their motives because I thought I knew everything. But not so much with Pops. I will never forget one time when I was hiking through the mountains in New Mexico with him and we came to a hill leading off into a pond. I loved being in the water and was eager to cool off after a hot day, so I asked Pops if I could jump in.

His response was short and blunt. "No."

I was a little taken aback and could think of only one retort. "Why not?"

My grandpa responded with a statement I will never forget. "Because you can trust me." I had no comeback for that. I could not tell him, "No, I can't trust you, so I'm just going to jump in." I trusted both his wisdom and his care for me more than anyone else I knew.

Seeing my disappointment, my grandpa walked me down the cliff to the pond and showed me why he had said no. He grabbed a stick and inserted it into the pond right under the edge of the cliff. It hit the bottom about four feet in. He jokingly said, "You see there. If you had jumped in, you would've broken your legs. Then your grandmother wouldn't cook for me anymore." It was a sweet moment when I learned even more that my grandfather's restrictions were based out of a love that wanted only the best for me. In his wisdom, he knew that what seemed right to me, what looked like a thrill, would end only in harm. He was more interested in my future wellbeing than in a current opportunity for a thrill.

What if a close friend, someone you trusted, told you they would give you one hundred dollars if you were able to do fifty pushups in a row? Now, fifty pushups in a row can be a difficult feat to accomplish for many people, and it would be easy to give up because of the pain and fatigue. But you would probably keep going.

Why would you be able to persist? Because you trusted that the person offering the reward would follow through. If you didn't know the person making the offer, you might be skeptical about the offer and decide to quit when the going got tough, having no motivation to keep pushing through the pain. In contrast, you knew your friend was dependable and trustworthy, and that they wouldn't make a guarantee they wouldn't keep.

Are you beginning to see the pattern in these stories? When we trust the person giving us instructions, or telling us we can't do something, obedience becomes much easier. Trust means we are confident the person has our best interests at heart, and we know the person will fulfill the promises they have made. That confidence means we have peace, knowing there is reason in our obedience, even if we don't immediately understand every reason.

Submission Sounds Weak

Now that we know we can trust God in our obedience, we'll be able to obey God in everything, right? Not really. Based on Scripture, we already know we are supposed to obey God. Obedience, however, doesn't always come easy, even though (as we've already discussed) we know God's promises are true. Have you ever played the game Mercy? You lock hands with your opponent and bend their fingers and hands until they beg for mercy. My friends and I played it often when we were growing up. It was not a game about fun—it was to establish dominance and identify who was weak that day. Whoever would submit first was considered feeble and would then have to endure a streamline of jokes about how funny their face had looked as they were begging for the other person to stop.

We never want to look weak in front of other people. We definitely don't like the idea of submitting to someone else. America preaches, "Don't do what everyone else thinks—just be you; be original." After all, submitting to what a person tells me to do makes me a weak person with no backbone, right? Of course, blindly following what others tell you to do is unwise. The problem is that the belief that we should never obey someone else carries over into our attitude toward God. We are so trained in being the Alpha in our own lives, that when it comes to obeying God, we struggle to hand over the reins. Deep down, our pride and arrogance fool us into thinking our ways are better than God's, that our understanding of the opportunity at hand is better than God's.

Give Me a Reason

But we have to begin reframing our thinking from trusting our own leadership to trusting God's leadership. Of course, when we are told to do something or not to do something, we want a good reason as to why. Asking God "why" is okay, but we need to know He isn't in the business of giving direct, detailed answers. He's in the business of building our faith in Him.

Proverbs 3:5-6

"Trust in the LORD with all your heart, and do not lean on your own understanding. In all your ways acknowledge him, and he will make straight your paths."

Hearing things like this from God isn't always easy because we want to know details, not general statements like "Trust in the LORD." What we can know from this is that God isn't telling us to find our own path, or to make things straight. He's instead communicating that if we'll just lean on Him more, we'll start to see how strong and able He is to effortlessly make our path straight. This is difficult to do, but this is a glorious promise from God that we can and should lean on when we want to ask, "Why, God?"

When we trust God and act in obedience, we are displaying a deep reliance on Him and the confidence we have in His care and faithfulness. Trusting in the Lord is more than just intellectual assent—it is necessary for our lives and our good. If I had been standing on that cliff in New Mexico with a stranger, I might have jumped into the pond, because I didn't know the man and had no prior relationship to give me reason to trust him. But since I was with my grandfather, someone who had shown me he had my best interests at heart, I obeyed him even though I wanted to jump. It is the same idea with God.

Obedience Results in Joy

There was a time in Jesus' life on earth when He chose joy. It was not in a moment where a thrill was offered, and it was not a time where fun or relaxation was offered. It was actually during His crucifixion:

Luke 22:42

"Father, if you are willing, remove this cup from me. Nevertheless, not my will, but yours, be done."

In the context of this verse, Jesus is with his disciples on the Mount of Olives, praying by Himself. His disciples were supposed to be praying as well, so that they would not enter into temptation, but they fell asleep. Now, Jesus, in the beginning of His prayer, asked His Father to take away the cup, the wrath of God. Why? Because Jesus knew what He was about to have to endure on the cross. Jesus was sinless, but would become sin. He knew He wasn't guilty, but He was going to represent the guilty before God, and that meant bearing His Father's wrath.

Luke 22:44

"And being in an agony he prayed more earnestly; and his sweat became like great drops of blood falling down to the ground."

Jesus was so distressed about having to undergo the wrath of God, He began to sweat blood. This condition is called hematidrosis, a very rare condition brought on from extreme stress in which humans sweat blood. Hematidrosis struck Jesus because He had the gut-wrenching weight of the world's sin on His shoulders, in front of a Holy God who accepts nothing less than perfection.

I had a friend growing up whom I will call John. John was the friend in our group who usually had the dumbest ideas. These ideas usually resulted in consequences for us, whether it was our parents finding out, the law getting involved, or someone getting hurt. I remember several times when John would be punished with a paddling. Every time John would be at odds with his parents' rules about something, it always ended with the paddle and a sore bottom for him. Though never once did I hear him say something like, "Please punish me, Mom, because I have disobeyed you." He always asked for mercy, and sometimes even attempted to bargain his way into a lesser punishment like timeout. John was terrified to face his mom when he had been disobedient.

Comparing John's fear of facing punishment to Jesus facing punishment is impossible, because John's mom, like every other human being, is neither perfect nor holy. And, of course, Jesus was not suffering because of an irresponsible act—He was suffering because He was taking the punishment of every sin that had been or would ever need to be atoned for. But this illustration can help us understand why Jesus asked God whether there was another way to atone for the sins of the world. Jesus understood the enormous weight He would have to bear. In an amazing act of love and trust, however, Jesus chose God's will, knowing that God's will was going to cost Him His life. Why did Jesus submit to God's will, even when it meant a gruesome death for Him?

Hebrews 12:2

"Looking to Jesus, the founder and perfecter of our faith, who for the joy that was set before him endured the cross, despising the shame, and is seated at the right hand of the throne of God."

Jesus endured the cross, and all of its physical pain, and underwent the wrath of God by taking upon Himself the sins of the world. Being crucified was designed to shame someone. Those being crucified were naked in public and suffered intense pain and humiliation. Why did Jesus submit to this? "For the joy that was set before Him!" This joy was something so amazing to Jesus that He, a sinless man, took on the sins of the world and suffered the worst death in history, so that joy could be His. The embraced promise of future reward was the joy that gave Jesus strength to suffer.

If I am able to trust that my grandfather's instructions were best for me, how much more then can I trust in God, my heavenly Father, who sent His son Jesus to die for me? Oh, so much more! If we believe our good in life is possessions and fulfilling our wants, obeying God will probably seem like the wrong path. Yet, when we know and trust that God has our best interests at heart, just as I trusted my grandpa wanted the best for me, we begin to build confidence that God's instructions are best.

The only way to truly tell if you can trust someone is to spend time getting to know them. Learn their personality, their characteristics, their integrity, and whether you can count on what they say. Over time, you will see a trustworthy person continually follow through on commitments, and you will note that they keep their word. Those consistent actions will build trust in your relationship.

The same truth applies to God. The only way we can know if we can count on His promises is by spending time with Him. Getting to know God means obeying Him.

The more we learn to trust in Him, the more we will step into obedience, because we are becoming more aware of what obedience is producing in us. More of God creates in us more joy, and displays to the world that we really trust in God, because as we get more of God we start feeling and knowing how satisfying He really is. As Christians, we must have faith in God, but faith is never grown from a life of answered questions. It is grown from a life that has no clue as to what is happening but acting in obedience, because we trust in God and His promises.

True Joy Comes from Praising God

In addition to obedience, part of the joy God gives us comes from our praising Him. Think of praise like a mountain with gold in it; the more we dig (praise) the more we discover. God's not playing hide and seek, or saying, "You have to do this in order to receive anything from me." Instead, He's led us to the mountain of himself. If God is our joy, why would we not dig to discover all we can to expand our joy in Him even more?

However, the Bible's instructions to praise God have, at times, confused people. In her late twenties, Oprah Winfrey left traditional Christianity because she was troubled when she heard that God is a jealous God. She, like many others, thought that God being a "jealous" God made Him sound as if He were needy, unsatisfied, and seeking the praise of man to feel good about Himself. In other words, God needed us to complete His joy. It can almost sound like someone who paints an amazing piece of art, and then proclaims, "Look at me, admire me, cherish me, praise me!"

Scripture further explains that God created the world for the praise of His glory and of His grace that was displayed in and through the death of Jesus. People sometimes do not like God's self-exaltation in a statement like this. It appears to some as if God demands praise because He needs people to make much of Him, and He craves attention. Seriously, when has God ever needed us? When was there a time in history that the creator was dependent on the creation for His own satisfaction? Never! God is completely satisfied because He is lacking nothing.

The problem with Oprah's belief about God is that she misunderstands why God would tell us to praise him. C.S. Lewis writes, "The miserable idea that God should in any sense need, or crave for, our worship like a vain woman wanting compliments, or a vain author presenting his new books to people who never met or heard him, is implicitly answered by the words, 'If I be hungry I will not tell thee' [Psalm 50:12]."[2]

In the quote above, Lewis writes only part of Psalm 50:12. The full verse is this: "If I were hungry, I would not tell you, for the world and its fullness are mine." At the time this verse was written, people were tempted to think that God needs sacrifices, and that they could bribe God to satisfy Him. God asks a rhetorical question here—there's no possibility that He's in need. We know from the Bible that God needs absolutely nothing: "The God who made the world and everything in it, being Lord of heaven and earth, does not live in temples made by man, nor is he served by human hands, as though he needed anything, since he himself gives to all mankind life and breath and everything"(Acts 17:24-25). The point is, if God were ever in need, He would never ask humans because we have no power or ability to help God in any way.

You might ask then, if God does not need us to praise Him, why would He be so passionate about it? I confess, I was confused about this question for a long time. At times, I was even reduced to tears because I felt as if everything I understood about God was untrue. My childhood faith had me believe God was for me alone, but hearing that He is for Himself made me feel like a slave who was just created to glorify God so He could be satisfied, even if it was at the expense of my happiness. Notwithstanding, everything about God's character opposes the belief that He wants our praise for Himself alone: His love for us, His constant forgiveness of us, and His sacrifice of his Son for us.

Think about John 3:16. That verse does not claim that "God so *needed* the world that He gave His one and only Son." It says that "God so *loved* the world that He gave His one and only Son." God sent His perfect Son to die for a people he loved, not a

---

2.   C. S. Lewis, *Reflections on the Psalms* (New York: Harcourt, 1986), 93.

people He needed. Think about the stunning reality of what God did for us. The people to whom God sent his perfect Son weren't people who showed great potential but were failures on every level. Imagine the worst sin or person you know right now. Is God's love unable to extend to them? Look at Paul. In 1 Timothy 1:15, Paul says, "The saying is trustworthy and deserving of full acceptance, that Christ Jesus came into the world to save sinners, of whom I am the foremost." Paul is the chief of sinners, and he's explaining here that no one else had "worse" sins than he did. God's grace, through Christ, extended to Paul, and therefore it can extend to the most vile, wicked person and acts you can think of. This is a love that is simply not comprehensible to humans. Would you let your child die for a murderer? I don't think I could, but God did. This is breathtaking. It's so amazing that when it grips you, you naturally fall into praise. You praise God for saving a self-condemned sinner like you who deserved His wrath but received His grace instead.

Even though we know God has saved us, sent His Son for us, and loves us more than we can grasp, it's easy to become caught up in daily life and stop seeing or acknowledging God's love. We don't live in the reality of God's love. When we praise God, however, we stop and consider what He has done for us. We acknowledge what He has done, is doing, and will do. We begin to connect with God and quiet the noise of life. Lewis further explains, "It is in the process of being worshiped that God communicates His presence to men. It is not of course the only way. But for many people at many times, the 'fair beauty of the Lord' is revealed chiefly or only while they worship Him together."[3] We can feel God's presence when we dwell on His goodness and praise Him.

Moreover, praise is not only a way to connect with God and see His love and goodness in a fresh way, but it is actually a natural effect of our love for Him and appreciation for what He

---

3.   C. S. Lewis, *Reflections on the Psalms*, 93.

has done for us. Any time we love something, we are excited to talk about it. Lewis explains,

> "I had never noticed that all enjoyment spontaneously overflows into praise unless . . . shyness or the fear of boring others is deliberately brought in to check it. The world rings with praise – lovers praising their mistresses, readers their favourite poet, walkers praising the countryside, players praising their favourite game. . . . Except where intolerably adverse circumstances interfere, praise almost seems to be inner health made audible. . . . I had not noticed either that just as men spontaneously praise whatever they value, so they spontaneously urge us to join them in praising it: 'Isn't she lovely? Wasn't it glorious? Don't you think that magnificent?' The Psalmists in telling everyone to praise God are doing what all men do when they speak of what they care about."[4]

When we are confronted with the all-satisfying beauty of God through Christ, we won't have a choice but to praise Him because we have seen and felt how satisfying and wonderful He is. It's a natural response.

Another natural response to what we love is that we feel a need to share what we love with other people. Lewis writes, "It is frustrating to have discovered a new author and not to be able to tell anyone how good he is; to come suddenly, at the turn of the road, upon some mountain valley of unexpected grandeur and then to have to keep silent because the people with you care for it no more than for a tin can in the ditch; to hear a good joke and find no one to share it with."[5] It feels disappointing, as Lewis relates , to be amazed at something but not have anyone to share

---

4.   C. S. Lewis, *Reflections on the Psalms*, 94.

5.   Ibid., 95.

it with or appreciate it as you do. For example, I am an avid golf fan and love to play the game. When young hotshot Jordan Spieth won the Masters in 2015, I was ecstatic. He is young and talented, making it easy to root for him to win the green jacket. I texted and called my friends and family who love golf and discussed his victory with them. I was not informing them of his win—I knew they had watched it. Instead, my excitement didn't feel complete until I was able to express it to others. It was even more enjoyable to praise Jordan's win with other people who shared in my enthusiasm. Even when I talked to friends who don't appreciate golf, I tried to invite them into my excitement by explaining to them why Jordan's win was a thrilling day. Whether they joined me in my excitement or not, they knew after talking to me that I was excited about Jordan Spieth.

Lewis shares, "The Scotch catechism says that man's chief end is 'to glorify God and enjoy Him forever.' But we shall then know that these are the same thing. Fully to enjoy is to glorify. In commanding us to glorify Him, God is inviting us to enjoy Him."[6] God commands us to praise Him, not because He is somehow incomplete without it, but because He is completing our joy by giving us His greatest gift, Himself, through our praise. God is our greatest good, so when He demands our praise of Him, He is loving us!

> "God's design to pursue his own glory turns out to be love. And our duty to pursue God's glory turns out to be a quest for joy."[7]
>
> —John Piper

---

6.   C. S. Lewis, *Reflections on the Psalms*, 96-97.

7.   John Piper, "God Is Most Glorified in Us When We Are Most Satisfied in Him," accessed July 21, 2016, http://www.desiringgod.org/messages/god-is-most-glorified-in-us-when-we-are-most-satisfied-in-him.

True Joy Comes from Treasuring Christ

One semester in college, I found something I badly wanted: a new guitar. I have played guitar since I was a little boy, and it is still a favorite hobby of mine. As I was standing in a music store perusing a music magazine, a guitar caught my eye. I didn't buy it that day, but I kept thinking about it. And the more I looked at it, researched it, and drooled over it, the more I felt I had to have it. I couldn't afford the guitar at the time, so I started saving money. I sorted through and gathered clothes, electronics, and anything I could to sell, and eventually gathered enough money to purchase the guitar. I was so impressed with this guitar that I knew I would later regret not having bought it. As soon as I saw it, I was in, no matter the cost.

This is the way seeing Christ and all that He is works. When we are drawn into Christ's beauty by seeing and understanding all that He is for us, our natural response is to treasure Him above all else, because we come into a joy that greatly surpasses anything else the world could offer us. We can't see Christ physically on this earth, but we are invited in to know Him through the Bible and the Holy Spirit. The more we see and understand of God, the more captivated we become.

Matthew 13:44

"The kingdom of heaven is like treasure hidden in a field, which a man found and covered up. Then in his joy he goes and sells all that he has and buys that field."

If you are familiar with this parable, you know that it is the shortest one in the Bible. The parable is only one verse, but it is such an explosive verse. One interesting aspect about the verse is that it does not describe any particular man at all. This man could be a rich man, a poor man, or a middle-class man. There are no restrictions to what your economic status has to be in order to find a treasure. That's amazing! This man was so blown away by the value of this treasure that he sold everything to purchase the land it was on, so that he could be the rightful owner. Nothing he owned was worth more to him than this treasure, and this treasure caused an immediate compulsive act, not a calculated act. And the act was one of joy.

Other than Christ, the Apostle Paul best displays for us that God is the most satisfying treasure in the entire world. Paul writes a letter to the Christians in the Roman colony of Philippi to encourage them in their commitment to God.

Philippians 1:20-23

"As it is my eager expectation and hope that I will not be at all ashamed, but that with full courage now as always Christ will be honored in my body, whether by life or by death. For to me to live is Christ, and to die is gain. If I am to live in the flesh, that means fruitful labor for me. Yet which I shall choose I cannot tell. I am hard pressed between the two. My desire is to depart and be with Christ, for that is far better."

What we can immediately see from the text is that the aim of Paul's life is to honor God's name because His name is great. We can also see that he wants this to happen in his life and in his death. Let's analyze how God is going to be seen as great in the life and death of Paul.

Great in Life

Philippians 3:8

"I count everything as loss because of the surpassing worth of knowing Christ Jesus my Lord. For his sake I have suffered the loss of all things and count them as rubbish, in order that I may gain Christ."

Everything Paul loves, possesses, and has done, is counted as a loss because of how much more knowing Christ surpasses it. He is not saying that all of these things are bad, but as soon as anything is compared with Christ, it instantly looks like rubbish to him, because the satisfaction of Christ easily surpasses anything else. In Paul's life, he is treasuring, esteeming, loving, and being satisfied with Christ so much so that anything that is not Him is rubbish when compared to Him. If everything is rubbish to Paul in comparison to Christ, then Christ is seen as the supreme treasure in Paul's life to the world.

Great in Death

Paul also makes clear that Christ will be honored in his death (Philippians 1:20). He also explains that, for him, death will be gain (Philippians 1:21), and he even desires to "depart" (that is, die) so that he can be with Christ (Phil 1:23). Paul shows a wonderful example of how our mind shifts when we start to value Christ above anything else. Instead of fearing or avoiding death, Paul actually considers death gain because he will be with Christ. He values Christ more than marriage, family, wealth, health, or reputation—an example that brings glory to Christ and is a strong testimony to the world.

There is another man mentioned in the Bible who had to sell all he had in order to inherit eternal life with Christ. This man is known as the rich young ruler, and his story is one of the saddest accounts in Scripture.

Matthew 19:16-22

"And behold, a man came up to him, saying, 'Teacher, what good deed must I do to have eternal life?' And he said to him, 'Why do you ask me about what is good? There is only one who is good. If you would enter life, keep the commandments.' He said to him, 'Which ones?' And Jesus said, 'You shall not murder, You shall not

*commit adultery, You shall not steal, You shall not bear
false witness, Honor your father and mother, and, You
shall love your neighbor as yourself.' The young man said
to him, 'All these I have kept. What do I still lack?' Jesus
said to him, 'If you would be perfect, go, sell what you
possess and give to the poor, and you will have treasure
in heaven; and come, follow me.' When the young man
heard this he went away sorrowful, for he had
great possessions."*

This man was eager to have eternal life. He called Jesus teacher and asked Jesus what needed to be done in order for him to inherit eternal life. When Jesus started listing off commands, this young ruler said that he had kept them all, and he did not know what he was missing. When Jesus revealed that eternal life is gained by selling all one has and following Christ, however, this young ruler left sorrowfully because he could not sell his great possessions. This ruler wanted life eternal, but he desired his possessions even more. This young ruler's treasure was not Jesus; it was his stuff.

It is heartbreaking when people do not receive Christ as the most beautiful, satisfying, fulfilling offer. As people seek happiness, they often turn away from Christ to run to something that does not have the capacity to satisfy them as Christ can. He is the most priceless and satisfying treasure there has ever been and ever will be, and the invitation to receive Him is an invitation to joy. Jesus is saying, "Do not settle for anything less than me. I am everything you have ever wanted in this life. Come to me, and drink from the fountain of my grace that never runs out and be satisfied." When we accept that offer, we are not only turning down the competing pleasures that this world has to offer us, but we are displaying to the world what we treasure most. This magnifies Christ and satisfies us completely, so much so that we can say with Paul that we are eager to be with Christ whether by our death or His second coming. We are all magnifying and treasuring something in our life. The question is, is it Christ, or is it some knock-off version of Him that tries to sound like Him, but fails to deliver?

*   *   *

My aim in the first few chapters of this book was to establish a foundation of what joy is and what it is not, so that you would have a clear understanding of what I am pleading with you to pursue. You might be asking the question, "I see now that God alone is my deepest joy, and I know joy stems from obedience, praise, and treasuring Christ. But how do I get more of God? What practical steps can I take to build joy into my life?" These are the questions we will answer in the rest of this book. In the chapters ahead, my aim is to help you fight for joy practically, emotionally, and spiritually.

> "God is most glorified in us when we are most satisfied in him."[8]
>
> —John Piper

---

8. John Piper, "God Is Most Glorified in Us When We Are Most Satisfied in Him," accessed July 21, 2016, http://www.desiringgod.org/messages/god-is-most-glorified-in-us-when-we-are-most-satisfied-in-him.

LIGHTS, CAMERA, ACTION

I hope that over the past few chapters you have come to believe that your most supreme joy comes from God alone. That happiness is good, but happiness is only circumstantial. That joy runs much deeper than happiness and is about contentment, hope, and trust in who God is and what He has promised to do.

In the coming chapters, we will discuss how to actively pursue joy. These methods help us know our Father more and develop more joy. They are essential for the Christian life and, without them, I do not believe we will ever know the joy of the Lord. Of course, these chapters do not cover every way to develop joy. However, these methods are some of the most essential approaches for all Christians if we want to become a people familiar with our God.

These chapters are NOT a checklist of things to do to be a good Christian, to earn God's favor, or to act "chipper" on a daily basis—they are disciplines taught in the Bible. Christians can very easily approach serving God as a list of dos and don'ts, so working to grow closer to God can sometimes feel like practicing a collection of religious acts. Besides, obedience to God, when done with the right understanding, is not legalism—it is worship. It is striving to know God better so that we can develop a deeper relationship with Him. Obedience is not worship when you submit simply because you're scared God might not give you what you want, or take away what you already have. Instead, we worship God by desiring Him in every aspect of our lives, and by understanding that obeying God is the path to knowing and desiring more of Him.

Implementing these practices into our lives isn't guaranteed to make us happy, because tragedy can strike at any moment whether we are walking with God or not. Regardless, these practices will lead you into a deeper relationship with God and help you understand His unconditional love for you. They will help turn your attention toward God, rather than working to get God's attention. The more you rely on God to be your source of joy, the more you'll start to see how the world and what it has to offer couldn't come close to satisfying you like God does.

As we ask God to change our hearts and minds, we must remember joy is not contingent on how we feel—it is contingent on our reliance on God and His wisdom. Through a life of obedience and of cultivating a heart that wants more of God, we will become a people who are joy filled instead of running aimlessly about seeking empty happiness. As you read through each chapter, ask God to deepen your personal relationship with Him, not by earning His favor, but by becoming more familiar with who He is and by enjoying His presence in your life.

SHEDDING A FEW POUNDS

This is not a chapter about health programs to get on in order to pursue joy. Most people will agree that being overweight is unhealthy—in fact, the weight loss industry nets billions of dollars every year because people want to shed weight. Losing weight can make you feel lighter, have more energy, and decrease the risks of inflammation, cancer, heart disease and many other health problems. Generally, many people don't realize that in our personal and work lives, most of us are also bloated. We're carrying around extra weight that is causing problems. But this kind of weight isn't physical; it is weight that hinders the pursuit of our joy in God.

The Bible instructs us as Christians to get rid of aspects of our lives that weigh us down. These are things that might not actually be weight to anyone else but ourselves. "Therefore, since we are surrounded by so great a cloud of witnesses, let us also lay aside every weight, and sin which clings so closely, and let us run with endurance the race that is set before us" (Heb. 12:1). This interesting verse in Hebrews speaks loudly to something highly overlooked in the Christian life. Look closely at the wording of the verse: "Let us also lay aside every weight, *and* sin which clings so closely." Do you see how the verse separates the "weight" from actual sin? This means that weights dragging us down will not necessarily be sin. Why are we instructed to lay aside some other category that is not sin?

God is warning us here that there can often be parts of our lives that hinder our walk with Him but are not actual sin. These weights can be anything at all, and are unique to each person. For example, during my junior year of college I went through a difficult period of time and sank into a deep depression. I could not sleep, could not eat, could not smile, and could not enjoy my friends. I was distraught. One thing I enjoy is music: rock, country, Christian rap, worship, coffee shop music, and so many more genres. I listen to music all the time; you will rarely find me without music playing. During that season of depression, I was of course listening to music often and, at first, I saw it as nothing more than just a part of my normal life.

Ultimately, I started to realize that some of the music I could usually enjoy suddenly became a trigger that would set off depression. Whether it was a lyric, a rhythm of instruments, or a certain song that brought a memory to mind, the music was dragging me down. So what did I do? As much as I hated to, I erased a lot of this music that triggered my sad emotions. I actually asked a dear friend of mine to erase the music for me so that I wouldn't have to. But I had to lay aside those songs because my brain and heart processed those songs in a way that pushed me away from trusting and loving Jesus. They hindered my run. While this sounded crazy to some of my friends (I even removed some of my worship music), I knew it was the right decision.

Laying aside these weights in our lives might seem silly to others, but anything that is a weight for us is not only important to remove, it is critical. If we want to commit to a lifelong pursuit of maximum joy in God, we must be willing to put things to death that weigh us down. When observing your own life and trying to determine what you need to decide, do not ask the question, "Is it a sin?" This attitude only tries to toe the line of sin and grace, and why would we toe that line? Instead, ask the question, "Is this aspect of my life robbing my affections for

God?" If we know our deepest joy is in Jesus, we will want to be a people willing to lose even the approval of other people, in order to grow closer to God.

If you are determining whether something is a sin, look only to the Bible. God's word helps you clearly identify what is and what is not specifically sin. But if you are putting parts of your life you know are not sinful to the test, you will need to look at yourself more closely to figure out whether or not certain aspects are helping you run your race more effectively. For me, when I put certain songs to the test, I knew fairly quickly they were weighing me down and preventing me from running. I had a choice to accept what I knew was killing me and continue in it, or to remove anything that turned me away from delighting in Jesus. I looked much more closely at music. Did it make me happy? Did it remind me of my depression? Did it make me enjoyable to be around? Did it make me cry? Did it spur me toward Jesus, or toward myself?

Consider the example of Usain Bolt. He is a Jamaican sprinter who is considered the fastest person who has ever run. He holds the 100 meter and 200 meter records and is the first man to win six gold medals in sprinting. I watched him run in the Olympics and was blown away at how fast he was. I knew he had committed to significant training and sacrifice and that he had trained religiously to get to where he was. When he set his goal to become world champion, he had to set aside many indulgences. I am sure he had to drink different drinks, eat different foods, and commit to many changes. If he was passionate about his goal, he did not care what others thought of him when he removed things from his life he had done in the past. He became so zoned in on his end goal that he would give up anything and implement action that would help him get there.

The Christian life is similar to that of an athlete. For Christians trying to gain more of Jesus, we have to be willing to get rid of anything that hinders our race toward Jesus, and implement aspects that spur us on to Jesus. As we strive to develop a deeper relationship with God, our reward will be great.

It Might Hurt

Some things we have to lay aside may even hurt us, but we have to be willing to pursue Jesus at the cost of our comfort. One year at a youth camp, I spoke with a young man who told me his testimony. He had been a drug addict, an alcoholic, a rebel, a thief, and would always get in trouble at school with his friends. He told me that when God saved him, life actually became harder for him. He struggled to stay away from drugs and alcohol, and his friends were not any help. When he tried to tell them about Jesus, they would shut him down, saying things like, "Just keep that Jesus stuff to yourself, Bro, when you're with us you're with us. Do that religious stuff on your own time." Their response put him in a hard position because he was pressed by Jesus to live a different lifestyle but his friends were all he had at the time. Eventually, one day he summoned courage to make one of the hardest decisions he had ever made: he faced his friends and told them he could not spend time with them anymore. He told them he knew God was not pleased with the life they were all living, and he could not be a part of it anymore. They responded harshly, saying, "You're such a hypocrite. You say you follow Jesus now, but didn't He run around with sinners? So, you think you're better than Him to get away from us. Go, hang out with those Christian friends of yours, because you're dead to us now."

When he told me this story, my heart broke for him because of the reaction from his friends. I thought about how I would feel if my friends ever rejected me. But was what he did hypocritical? After all, Jesus did hang out with sinners. Nonetheless, this young man's decision was not hypocritical because the group of guys he had run around with his whole life was not helping him run his race. He told me, "Being around those guys was like hanging myself. I couldn't breathe and felt helpless." He was willing to let go of people, because the life they lived didn't give life to him—it took life away from him. He wanted Jesus, not the approval of friends. Friends are not inherently evil, but even friends can become a weight.

Addressing Legalism

Removing weights from your life can be a tricky road to navigate. Because of our deceitful hearts and minds, we could be carrying so much weight that we are barely moving, but we might mistakenly believe we are running the race pretty well. Something that is life-giving for others could actually be poison for you. As a result of these differences, people can sometimes view us as legalistic because we remove certain aspects from our lives. They don't understand why we need to abstain from an action, when that same action is not a problem for them. People might call you self-righteous, hypocritical, judgmental, ignorant, and many other names for avoiding things they might be consuming. Even Christians might see you as legalistic because these weights are not specifically sin, but you have made them sin by treating them as a part of your life you cannot do without.

Our concern as Christians needs to be more about following the Bible than coming off as legalistic to the world. What if I would have never left the music that was dragging me down? I might still be depressed, trying to heal but feeling as if I were cut open again when I listened to the wrong music. I would have had no progress in my growth with Jesus because I was more concerned about legalism than clinging to Him.

As we work to rid our lives of the weights that hinder us, it can be tempting to let the world know about the changes we're making in order to be seen as some sort of elite Christian. I confess that I've been guilty of the infamous "humble brag." I had done something in the name of God, and I felt like people needed to know about it. For example, I recently deleted social media from my smart phone because I felt like it was making me anxious and that I was spending too much time on it. After taking out the social media, though, I soon realized I was letting everyone know about what I had done because I wanted people to see me as the guy who was pursuing God really well. But in reality, I took something God had intended to stir my affections for Him and I used it for my own glory.

What is Weighing You Down?

So what is it in your life that is weighing you down? Maybe it is a job, a relationship, music, movies, food, or shopping. My hope and desire for you is that you would start putting things in your life to the test. Ask yourself whether your actions help or hinder your run. If your weight is not a sin but is hindering your run, I hope you have an eager desire to lay it down regardless of whether it did not affect you in the past. Let us be a people willing to lay down anything that would get in our way of pursuing Jesus. Let us be a people willing to be mocked by the world for relentlessly pursuing Jesus. If Jesus is the height of our pleasure and joy, then laying down anything for more of Him is necessary for our own souls.

THE GREAT 18

While I haven't been shy about my love of golf in this book, this chapter is not about eighteen holes on a golf course. This is a chapter about the most important eighteen inches that exist. These are the eighteen inches that mark the distance from your head to your heart. You might be wondering how this area can be more important than other organs. Well, these eighteen inches have to do with spiritual warfare. This warfare is more dangerous than cancer, stealthier than a snake, and aims to steal our joy in God.

Where the Battle Starts

Before we ever commit to anything, we first process it in our minds. From the food we eat to the thrills we seek, our minds process and decide every action we make, even if just for one second. When I am offered dinner from a friend, my heart is not set on it until I run it through my mind, and decide whether or not I am excited about it. Sin works the same way in our lives. A person is tempted, thinks about it, and either commits to sin or commits to not sin. I used to think my sin problem was only an issue of not being able to resist temptation but, when I started tracing back my sin to its initial starting point, I always wound up in my own mind. Sin is a process—it is not immediate. Sin happens after we have meditated on the temptation long enough to convince ourselves to sin, whether it takes one hour or just one second.

We have to understand that sin happens because we do not capture temptation as soon as it enters the mind and challenge it with truth. The person who is upset at someone else is bitter only because they have let negative thoughts about the other person continue to stir in their mind and create more reasons to be angry. The spouse who commits adultery does not just sleep with another person, they brood on thoughts of how pleasurable, enjoyable, and thrilling it would be until they are convinced the risk is worth it, despite the cost of their infidelity.

Growing up, I felt like my mother was never for me. I believed she took the side of other people. She would consistently pose a response of "maybe" to my relentless efforts to convince her of my perspective of a situation. My mother did believe me, but she wanted me to see a different perspective instead of being stuck on one thought or idea. What I see now is that my mom was training me from a young age to learn that my first initial thoughts might not always be right or even good, and I might need to consider an alternative perspective.

Satan wants us to believe in the initial thoughts of temptation, that whatever our thoughts are, they need to be carried out. He solicits our mind to stir the affections of our heart to get us to sin. For example, when Satan tempted Jesus in the wilderness, he continually appealed to Jesus' intellect in order to affect Jesus' emotions (Matthew 4:1-11). But Jesus was able to respond to these temptations with God's word. We have to make a conscious decision to transfer a temptation from our thoughts down into our hearts—our emotions and feeling. We have to decide to commit to the thought. If we do not have truth to combat those impulses that will not lead us to joy in God, we will continually run to sin in our own broken wisdom.

Aimless Consumption

Basically, we should understand that we must have a firm grasp of God's truth in order to practice discernment about our lives. In a world full of deceptive marketing, distinguishing what is beneficial and what is harmful for us can prove difficult. Every marketing ad is geared toward bettering ourselves. Take this vitamin, get this new phone with the fancy camera, eat this type of food, experience this thrill, and the list goes on. Imagine someone going to a buffet with a blindfold on. They could end up eating food they might be allergic to, do not like the taste of, or has no benefit to a diet they're on. Just because a person is hungry does not mean any kind of food would benefit them.

I know I am quick to rush from one event to the next in life. I feel as if I need the next "it" item to stay up to date with society, social status, or to have the approval of those around me. I hardly ever actually take a deeper look into anything that extends past a commercial or article in a magazine. But what I have realized is that I have been buying into anything and everything and becoming an aimless consumer. And here is the interesting part: it is rarely the item I am attached to, it is what that item provides me with that I try to hold onto.

If we could wake up every morning and not have to do anything to get the satisfaction we want, we would most likely just stay in bed all day. We all have desires that are physical and emotional, but the means we use to satisfy them can be poisonous to us without even realizing it. If we are going to live a life pursuing our joy in God, we must become more aware of how our heads and hearts work together to be able to distinguish what and what not to consume.

Don't Believe Everything You Think

One of the best ways for us to fight sin and pursue joy is by waging war on the mind. Why? Because our minds are the first step towards fighting sin. If we do not have a skillful strategy to govern our minds, they will constantly send our hearts poison to indulge in.

I am a person who is very quick to run with thoughts in my mind. I can be immersed in a good book, have a random thought in my mind, and in fifteen seconds be lost in bitterness, lust, envy, pride, self-exaltation, greed, or self-righteousness. Perhaps you can relate. Think about how easy it is for us to take an innocent thought and within seconds turn it into sin. If that processed thought were displayed on a projector to a crowd full of people, how embarrassed and ashamed we would all be. If the majority of my thoughts throughout the day were exposed to the world, I would find the closest place to hide my face. We are foolish to think we do not need to worry much about our minds and what we allow to freely run through them. It is just as dangerous as dancing on a cliff edge thinking we will not fall because we know where the precipice is. What happens when the cliff begins to crumble? We must not become familiar with the line of sin; we must instead become familiar with the desire we have to toe the line and kill that desire. Why would we want to do as much as we can without sinning instead of doing all that we can to know God all the more? We are not wise to run aimlessly with our minds, thinking we can flirt with temptation but won't sin. We need to actively destroy thoughts in our heads that are gateways for sin.

Become a Preacher

From the time you wake up in the morning until you go to bed, someone is talking to you. Do you know who it is? It is you. No one talks to you more than yourself. In Martyn Lloyd Jones's book, he says,

> Have you realized that most of your unhappiness in life is due to the fact that you are listening to yourself instead of talking to yourself? Take those thoughts that come to you

the moment you wake up in the morning. You have not originated them, but they start talking to you, they bring back the problems of yesterday, etc. Somebody is talking. Who is talking? Your self is talking to you.[9]

I believe what Jones wrote is true. When I think about times of sadness, frustration, depression, or pride, I have arrived there because I listened to my own thoughts. If my own thoughts take me to places that are not peaceful, something is wrong with me. What I need is another word that is not my own. What I need is God's word.

In Psalm 42, David has been listening to his own thoughts and soul. His thoughts have been crushing him and making him more depressed. What David does because of this is start a conversation with himself.

Psalm 42:11

"Why are you cast down, O my soul, and why are you in turmoil within me? Hope in God; for I shall again praise him, my salvation and my God."

David initiated a conversation with himself by literally speaking to himself. It sounds a bit weird, right? David might even sound like a crazy man, since he is talking to someone who is not there, but he was not crazy. David had been listening

---

9.   Dr. Martin Lloyd-Jones, *Spiritual Depression: Its Causes and Cures* (London: HarperCollins, 1965), https://books.google.com/ books?id=Grk7CwAAQBAJ&printsec=frontcover&source =gbs_ ge_summary_r&cad=0#v=onepage&q=Have%20you%20 realized%20that%20most%20of%20your%20unhappiness%20 in%20life%20is%20due%20to%20the%20fact%20that%20 you%20are%20listening%20to%20yourself%20instead%20 of%20talking%20to%20yourself%3F%20&f=false.

to his own thoughts that had been stealing away his peace, so he started to speak to himself about God. David became a preacher. What he initially said was, "Soul, I've listened to you long enough, and now I've got something to say to you." He knew that his own thoughts were insufficient to set his hope on God, so he started preaching truth into his own mind, fighting his fleshly thoughts and beliefs that had led him to depression.

Assess Yourself

One thing we can do is imitate David when dealing with thoughts that rob our joy in God. This practice starts by actively observing yourself. If you are not on guard about what is in your head, you are a sitting duck for sin. I talk to myself often whether I am driving, getting ready in the mornings, exercising, or any activity where my thoughts run rampant. I probably look like I have an imaginary friend to others, if they see me doing it. I ask myself all the time, "Soul, why are you sad?" or I tell myself, "Soul, that's a dumb thought and it's not true."

Assessing yourself might feel awkward, but it has to be done. For example, pretend as if you are at a doctor's office because you have a cold. When the doctor asks you "What's going on with you today?" and you respond, "I don't know," that would be a waste of time and money. In order to get better from the cough, you need to let the doctor know you actually have a cough. It is their job to treat you appropriately to fight something that is harming you.

This is the same concept as preaching to yourself. You have to first realize the problem, and that comes from your assessing yourself and figuring out why you're troubled, and why your soul, like David's, was cast down. Bother yourself with questions until you can accurately trace what thoughts and beliefs are robbing your joy. It could be anything in the world, but you will only come to know what the root of it is when you become honest with yourself and answer, "I'm cast down because …" After you've answered truthfully, you can then take the next step toward joy.

Speak Truth to Your Soul

Think of the example of the doctor's office again. When the doctor asks what is wrong and you tell him you have developed a persistent cough, the doctor will most likely know what medicine to give to you. The medicine will be tailored to what you need instead of a random guess that might not help at all.

After we have assessed ourselves, we should do what David did and preach truth to our souls: "Your Father is God, the sovereign King who looks after you, who doesn't allow anything to come into your life without His approval. Hope in Him." Or, "If you really believe this, you are making grace seem like it's based on merit. Look to the cross of Jesus. Trust that His death was enough to please the wrath of God." Or, "Fight hard, God will sustain you."

If you think that as soon as you speak truth to yourself all of your temptations, struggles, and fears go away immediately, you will soon figure out you are mistaken. This battle in the mind is a never-ending warfare. This is a conflict that will not go away until we are with Jesus, either by death or by his second coming. The fight of the Christian to put their faith and hope in Jesus Christ every day was never promised to be easy. This is combat.

What soldier enlists in the military thinking that battles will be be non-confrontational, easy, and comfortable? Rather, soldiers understand that war is nasty, violent, harmful, and deadly. We as Christians need to understand that the battle in the mind, if fought well, will bear resemblances to a physical war. Sometimes we need to get violent against our own thoughts and fight them at the first sight of lies. We know from David that preaching to ourselves is necessary. It's part of our pursuit of joy; training our minds to fight thoughts that won't lead us to more affection for God helps our joy in God become more consistent. So how do we know what we need to preach to ourselves? How do we figure out which medicine to prescribe to ourselves for a specific sickness? These questions lead us into the next chapter.

BIBLE, BIBLE, BIBLE

We will never go to the Bible until we are convinced that we need to. If something is not necessary, it becomes optional. If we think the Bible is not essential, we have deceived ourselves into thinking we will be just fine without it. How can anyone wanting to follow Jesus be fine without reading the Bible? We can't! The Bible is God's very word. We need to become familiar with what He has spoken if we want to be able to pursue our joy in Him alone.

The Bible Is Not a Blog

Something that has become very popular in today's society through social media is blogging. A good number of these blogs are written by someone who thinks that what they say is fact, but they mostly are just a few pages loaded with personal emotion. Please, do not hear me say that blogging is bad. I am an active blogger, and my goal in writing a blog is to always write something that will stir the affections of people to desire more of Jesus in some way. Inevitably, as blogs became more popular, I found myself reading blog after Christian blog. Some were good and some were terrible, but I was always looking for the one with the best title, best background, and best theme. I began browsing through blogs during my time I had set aside to be with the Lord. The problem was that I was getting my fill of God, emotional desire to live for Him, and relief from stress, from the words of others. I relied on these people to excite me about God, rather than the very words of God Himself.

2 Timothy 3:16-17

"All Scripture is breathed out by God and profitable for teaching, for reproof, for correction, and for training in righteousness, that the man of God may be complete, equipped for every good work."

Scripture affirms that every single word in the Bible is from God—making Scripture the highest authority—and all of the Bible is beneficial in some way. The Bible also helps us grow and equips us for good works.

Hebrews 4:12

"For the word of God is living and active, sharper than any two-edged sword, piercing to the division of soul and of spirit, of joints and of marrow, and discerning the thoughts and intentions of the heart."

Incredibly, the word of God is not just a historical document, but it is actually living, active, and sharper than any sword. God uses verses to expose a person's thoughts and intentions. Blogs, books, sermons, devotionals and so on might be influenced by God's word, but they should not be replacing God's word in our lives.

Don't Settle for Indirect Knowledge

If I wanted to know someone, I could research them extensively, ask questions about them from others familiar with that person, and maybe even read a book about them. Candidly, if I had the opportunity to know that person from meeting them face to face, talking with them, learning their characteristics, and watching them live life, how foolish would I be to settle for an article written about them? That article would benefit me, but how much more would I benefit from sitting down with the person one on one and learning about them firsthand?

Imagine if someone was working for Facebook and never met Mark Zuckerberg, Chairman and CEO of Facebook. They heard about him only from his peers and were told many conflicting reports: that he was driven, nice, mean, greedy, giving, pompous, or humble. Some of those reports might be true and some of them might be false, but the only way to know for sure would be for that individual to personally meet and get to know Mark Zuckerberg. They would need to meet him, hang out with him on a regular basis, and figure out who he really is. And while many employees at Facebook most likely won't be able to know Zuckerberg on a personal level, we have the opportunity to know God on an intimate level through His word.

One of the reasons we need to be active readers of the Bible is so we can learn more about Him for the purpose of discerning what others say about Him. If someone does not know the story of Jesus healing a blind man and is told that one of Jesus' disciples actually healed the blind man, they would ignorantly believe a lie. Hear this: ignorance is not stupidity. It is a lack of knowledge or information. For us, being ignorant of God is no excuse in the Christian life. If we say, "we didn't know," it is not because we did not have access to knowledge, because we do. We have simply not valued God's word as the primary source of our knowledge of Him and the authority over our lives. This willful ignorance is often seen in those who believe the prosperity gospel. People believe that if they meet certain standards on a checklist, God will bless them materialistically. They think their actions bring God's blessings into their lives when, in reality, it's only the blood of Christ. These falsehoods happen when our attention wanders from Scripture: everything we read or hear outside the Bible about God and living as a Christian can and should be tested within the Bible alone.

Luke 10:27

"And he answered, "You shall love the Lord your God with all your heart and with all your soul and with all your strength and with all your mind."

We are told to love God with all our heart, soul, strength, and mind. How do we love God with all our mind? By putting forth the effort, whether it be hard or easy to understand God, through His word. We cannot expect to just podcast our way to understanding God alone. We need to be a people with a radical pursuit of loving God with our minds. Studying the Bible and the complexities that arise within it can easily be frustrating. We are guarding our minds from lies, however, when we grind through the task of dissecting difficult Scripture. Part of our pursuing joy in God means a deeper understanding of who He is and what He has to say about our lives. Let's read and study the Bible actively to become more knowledgeable, so we can stand ready with truth when falsehood about God or certain aspects about Scripture arise. Let's be ready to give an account for the hope that is within us (1 Peter 3:15).

Memorizing Scripture

Memorizing Scripture is crucial for the Christian and is one of the most essential disciplines we need to learn.

Psalm 119:9, 11

"How can a young man keep his way pure? By guarding it according to your word. . . . I have stored up your word in my heart, that I might not sin against you."

These two verses, and many others (Joshua 1:8, Jeremiah 15:16, Colossians 3:16, Psalm 37:1, etc.) are motivations for us to memorize the word of God. Knowing that my conduct, character, and devotion to God is spurred on through His word is a massive motivation for me to memorize Scripture.

Preaching to ourselves, as discussed in the last chapter, is a weapon to fight sin, lies, heavy heartedness, bitterness, and so on. However, what do we preach to ourselves? How do we know what is in the midst of the chaos of our thoughts? We cannot use wisdom from people who do not know or desire God; instead, we need to use the truth from God's word.

Memorizing Scripture enables us to immediately respond to temptation and sin with words from the very mouth of God. What words could be more powerful than God's words? When we are tempted to sin in our minds, we can combat those thoughts by loading our minds with thoughts of God. I am not going to tell you which verses to memorize, because the Bible would confirm that they are all profitable, but I will give you an example of what it looks like to actively use God's word to help pursue joy in God.

Let's say a friend of mine offends me by talking behind my back, and I hear about what he said. My initial reaction is to be angry, talk bad about him, and then call him to make him feel bad about what he said. These are the immediate thoughts being processed in my head. If I dwell on these thoughts for even a short period of time, they can easily sink into my heart and tempt me to act out of my sinful emotion. But if I start preaching God's word into my mind and heart when those thoughts are rushing in, I have a greater truth to act on. So I will memorize this verse:

Ephesians 4:31-32

"Let all bitterness and wrath and anger and clamor and slander be put away from you, along with all malice. Be kind to one another, tenderhearted, forgiving one another, as God in Christ forgave you."

My own flesh is telling me to act in anger, but God would tell me to counter my bitterness with forgiveness, remembering how Christ forgave me.

If I am not convinced I need to forgive my friend, I will repeat this verse in my mind:

Proverbs 3:5-6

"Trust in the LORD with all your heart, and do not lean on your own understanding. In all your ways acknowledge him, and he will make straight your paths."

Trusting in the Lord is the only way to live a wise life. In that moment of wanting to lash out toward my friend, I will refrain because of the Ephesians verse. If I still think I should lash out, I can tell myself I need to trust in the Lord and not act out of emotion. I should practice self-control over my tongue and ask the Lord to give me the grace to truly forgive my friend. This trusting in the Lord and not my own understanding is an action that will guide me to a deeper faith in God, creating a deeper reliance in His care and faithfulness to His word over my life. This practice gives me more joy, because I then learn and experience more of God, my greatest good. I am pursuing joy by trusting God. After I have decided to acknowledge God over my emotion, I can then glorify God by showing how He has given me victory. I urge you to see memorizing Scripture, not as a weekly task to show your friends how smart you are, but as a way to engage your mind against the enemy and build deeper reliance on God's desire for you to be satisfied completely in Him.

But What if I Don't Feel Like Reading the Bible?

There have been times in my life when reading the Bible felt so empty. I would read the Gospels and feel bored, with no enjoyment, thrill, or pleasure in anything I had just read about

Jesus. I felt dry and had little desire to seek life from the Bible. This feeling was very discouraging for me. I would sometimes think I was not even truly a Christian because I lacked a desire to read the Bible. Perhaps you can relate to this. As you read this book, you agree with what has been said, but you have zero motivation to actually put any of it to action. What do you do?

We need something inside of us that will work in our hearts to see Jesus Christ as supremely beautiful on a day-to-day basis. When we are moved to see Jesus in our hearts as the height of our delight, all of the pleasures of the world lose their "pleasurableness" inside of us, and by reaction we will run to the most pleasurable source in the universe, Jesus Christ. We will go to the Bible to learn about Him for more pleasure of Him. This is the work of the Holy Spirit, and we should beg God to restore in us the joy of our salvation (Psalm 51:12) as we read the Bible. We should plead with God to open our eyes again to the beauty of Jesus and to have an explosive passion to come to Him to satisfy our thirst.

Isn't That Hypocritical?

You might think I am telling you to force yourself to read the Bible when you do not want to, and I am. I am not telling you to do this as a hypocrite. You can read the Bible when you do not want to read it without being hypocritical.

Hypocrisy when reading the Bible is studying it when you do not desire to, but appearing to those around you as if you do not lack a desire to know God and know His word. Then you have lied to the community around you, because they think that when you are reading the Bible, you actually want to do so.

The alternative is honesty. You have to be honest with yourself that you don't want to read God's word and know Him through it. You then invite people into your life by confessing your lack of desire to read the Bible, and asking them to pray for your desire to know God again. In addition, tell God how you feel—you won't surprise Him! He already knows you lack that desire (Psalm 139:2). We must get honest with God and others about the desire we want but do not have, and plead with God to move in our hearts to give us joy as we read through His mighty word.

We should be reading the Bible so that we may come to a deeper knowledge, love, and joy in Him. In doing so, during those seasons where we lack a desire to know God, we have to understand this world is actively trying to steal that desire. We have to get honest with where we are, read the Bible even if the zeal is not there, ask people to pray for us, and cry out to God to chisel the stone-like heart out of us. That is not hypocrisy; that is honesty.

SET A TIME!

This aspect is highly important! In the world where we live, we are always busy. This world has so much for us to do during the day that, if we do not find a specific time to set aside to read the Bible, we never will. I am sure you can understand this. I have ADHD, and I can easily have great intentions about reading the Bible but still struggle to follow through. If I am not extremely committed, something else will usually consume that time.

I am a morning person; I love getting up early and starting the day off being productive. This is the time of day I read the Bible. It works well because I have fewer distractions. You might not be a morning person, and that is okay. Figure out a time during the day when you can set aside all distractions, and spend time with God in His word.

We can easily create excuses to not read the Bible, but when we understand how necessary the word of God is for us each day, we understand how much more essential it is for us to go to it during the day. Throughout the day, we need food to function well, both mentally and physically. When we read the Bible, we are eating spiritual food, and we need it daily to continually put our hope and trust in Jesus Christ.

When we have a set time throughout the day to read the Bible, we need to focus only on the Bible. Something I absolutely have to do is turn my cell phone off. I know that if it starts alerting me, I will quickly be looking at a notification, texting, or surfing the web. These are small but common distractions for Satan to use against us to take our concentration off of God and re-focus it onto something that seems so innocent. For example, if you are at dinner with someone, you should listen with intentionality to what they are saying. If they are talking and you are looking off, texting, or playing a game, they will most likely feel disrespected. It is the same with God. Read His word, let Him speak to you, and do not treat Him like He is just another "thing" on your to-do list for the day. If God is our joy, reading His word will lead us into a deeper relationship with Him as we come to understand even more about God Himself. God chiefly speaks to us through His word, and we need the Bible as a window to look out into the vast beauty of God to satisfy our souls like nothing else in this world can. After all, through the Bible, God is offering us the greatest gift ever—a life which includes more of God Himself.

DON'T FAKE IT TILL YOU MAKE IT

It Starts Early

Growing up, I was blessed to have some amazing friends. I cannot recall any big event in my life when my friends were not with me. Whether we were getting into trouble for being reckless, or just celebrating birthdays, we were always together. We all lived in the same neighborhood, so we had daily access to each other in a matter of minutes. If we ever wanted to hang out, we did not have to get our moms to drive us; we would either ride our bikes or walk to each other's houses.

You would think we knew everything about one another, that our secrets were the group's secrets, and that if we were questioned about anyone in the group, we would make a 100. As I look back on my childhood, though, I realize the only information we would tell each other was information that made us look good, built us up, and made us more popular or more cool. We never exposed anything that would make us look weak, weird, or un-cool, because growing up was all about exalting ourselves to our peers in order to fit in.

We were never told we should be honest and expose things that might give people a reason to not consider us cool anymore. We were told through peers, TV, magazines, and Sports Center that we needed to strive to be the best we could be, and fake it 'till we made it.' We believed exposing weaknesses made us weak and that weaknesses should be dealt with privately in isolation. We believed that bringing our problems to someone else was selfish.

From a very young age, we were taught that the only way we could add value to society is by bringing it our best and keeping out our worst. If we are to influence lives, make a difference in our generation, and excel, we should expose the best qualities and traits we have to offer, and the ones that do not add value, simply ignore them and pretend you do not have any faults. Undeniably, bringing the real you with real problems and sins to God and others is part of the path to freedom and joy in God. You're never going to get any better by pretending you're always okay.

High School Accountability

One year in high school, two of my best friends and I decided to become accountability partners. We met up at Dairy Queen with our youth pastor, and he walked us through a document statement that was basically an agreement that we would meet up regularly, read the Bible together, pray for one another, and confess sin. It sounded great, looked great, and was great to practice, but my friends and I had been trained from a very young age to have it all together. So even though we signed this agreement, nothing about our lives and our friendship changed.

We met up frequently and would ask things like, "So what have you been struggling with?", "What has God been teaching you?", and so on. It was short, easy, and comfortable. I would catch myself lying sometimes, because I did not want to expose my weakness. I would tell them that I was reading the Bible when I was not, and that I was praying when I was not. Most of the time, when I tried to tell the truth, it was only a half-truth. Instead of telling them I was looking at porn frequently, I would just tell them I was struggling with lust. I became a pro at telling half-truths, because I believed that, if they knew the full truth, I would be exposed, cast out, and my life would be over.

I love those friends of mine greatly, but we would all now agree our accountability was not true accountability. We did not know what it meant to confess sin, because as far as we knew, sin was bad, and being bad was a hush-hush subject. We never had anyone to model for us what true accountability meant, especially from living in a small town, where everyone knew everything about you.

Exposed and Embraced

Being raised to believe that we cannot expose ourselves to others can actually move us into believing that we cannot expose ourselves to God. That He will only accept us, consider us cool, and want us around, if we only bring to Him our best selves. What that looked like for me was being involved at church, praying at night, reading the Bible, and giving money to the poor. I knew there was nothing I could do that God was not aware of, so I did all of these things out of fear that God would not accept me and would cast me into hell. These acts were never genuine; they were a feeble effort to find favor with God. If I did good deeds, I figured I did not have to talk to God about my sins and He would overlook them because of my good deeds.

But thinking that I had to do more to earn more favor from God was a lie. I had not yet realized that Christ's death on the cross was an exchange; Christ's righteousness was given to me, and my unrighteousness was placed on Christ (2 Corinthians 5:21). How crazy it is that Christ literally died for our sins so that God would accept us—not because we are righteous, but because of Christ's righteousness! This truth blows me away every day.

1 John 1:9

"If we confess our sins, he is faithful and just to forgive us our sins and to cleanse us from all unrighteousness."

We learn from Scripture that we can expose our sinful selves to God, ask for forgiveness, and be cleansed. Some of us think that it stops there, that only God needs to see our dirty deeds, because He is the only one who will accept us and because He accepts His son who represents us. But what if God commanded us to tell people who are just as sinful as us about our sins? We would have to become counter-cultural and let people know how uncool we are. It would mean that everything we have grown up believing about our weaknesses needing to be hidden is a lie, and we will have to accept being rejected in some cases. You see, God desires for us to confess our sins, struggles, and shortcomings to fellow believers. If God is telling us to confess sins to one another, it's for the ultimate purpose of our falling more in love with God.

College Accountability

When I went to college, I began to learn more about true accountability. There I pledged to a Christian fraternity, whose pledge process was the hardest event I have ever gone through because of how uncomfortable it made me feel. I remember going into the fraternity thinking I would look cool and would be ready for it because I had done accountability in high school. Boy, was I wrong.

First, we learned about confession, what it meant, and how God intended to use it as a means to help us become more godly. Our pledge captains harped one night on this verse:

James 5:16

"Therefore, confess your sins to one another and pray for one another, that you may be healed. The prayer of a righteous person has great power as it is working."

I heard this and felt a bit awkward and timid, but thought to myself that it would be something in which we all say we struggle with pride, lust, and selfishness. Then, we would pray for God to help us become more humble, to control our eyes and thoughts, and to become more selfless.

On one of the first nights when my fraternity brothers and I were hanging out, one of them asked me a question that made me feel attacked. He asked what my struggle was, and when I told him lust, he asked, "How so?" *Now, hold on,* I thought. *I told you lust, but you are not supposed to ask me details, and I am most certainly not supposed to give them. Right?* I replied, "Umm, just, you know, checking out girls." He then asked, "Have you been looking at pornography?" *Okay, he has crossed the line,* I thought. *Who is this guy to assume and even have the audacity ask me if I have been looking at porn?* Although I was taken aback by his boldness, his questions would begin to help me reach a level of honesty I had never reached before. I realize now, four years later, that this person was a brother who loved me enough to ask questions whose answers my flesh would be quick to hide.

Follow Directions

What good was it to anyone if I just kept telling a half-truth? Covering up my sin was not doing me any good, and it certainly was not helping anyone in my life to know what to pray for me, what questions to ask me, and how to respond to what I would tell them. What I did not see was that my sin was worse than I made it out to be. I thought sin was just a cold that would eventually pass with moderate attention; when in reality, it is a cancer that needs serious attention—attention that extends beyond my logic and into biblical obedience.

Think about when you are prescribed a medicine or you pick something up over the counter. What is the first thing you do when you get it? You read the directions. Why do you follow those directions? Because you trust that the person who wrote them knows how to properly take the medicine. So, you follow directions for healing. The Bible also offers us directions, but these directions give life instead of just curing a cold. We need to look to biblical directions for our deathly infections. When God says we need to confess our sins and pray for one another, we need to do just that because there is healing in that process.

Romans 8:13

"For if you live according to the flesh you will die, but if by the Spirit you put to death the deeds of the body, you will live."

The Spirit's power is what helps us put sin to death, but we have to take an active role in fighting our sin. If you think you can fight sin without confession, I have to ask you, "How is that going?" How is that "I'll do it tomorrow" promise going? How is that New Year's resolution to stop looking at porn going? How is gambling, the broken marriage, self-abuse, swearing, abusing alcohol or drugs, and on and on, going? My guess from experience and hearing many testimonies is that things are possibly not going great at all. You make promises to yourself you know you cannot keep. You believe you have enough will power to just white knuckle what you have been losing to for days, months and even years.

Here is the good news. God never intended us to white knuckle our lives. He intended us to live in community no matter our circumstances on earth.

Acts 2:42-47

"And they devoted themselves to the apostles' teaching and the fellowship, to the breaking of bread and the prayers. And awe came upon every soul, and many wonders and signs were being done through the apostles. And all who believed were together and had all things in common. And they were selling their possessions and belongings and distributing the proceeds to all, as any had need.

And day by day, attending the temple together and breaking bread in their homes, they received their food with glad and generous hearts, praising God and having favor with all the people. And the Lord added to their number day by day those who were being saved."

These verses are a beautiful proof that we as Christians are not supposed to live in seclusion. We are supposed to live in life-embracing community. When we have a community of believers around us who are interested in our love and growth toward God, and we are interested in theirs as well, no sin we confess will cause anyone to judge us, cast us out, or call us names. Rather, we can expect more encouragement, more accountability, more help, more prayer, and more truth being spoken over us. Then, we can follow directions with the belief that we need people in our lives to know our sinfulness, because our sins were what crucified Jesus.

If we desire to grow in our relationship with God, we have to stop acting as if we're okay. That is exactly what we do when we do not confess our sins or just stay on the surface with them. We set ourselves up to never get better, but to continue getting more and more sick. Sin is not a small "thing" you can "deal with." It is deadly. We need to treat it by following directions God has given us. Let's purpose to be a people of confession, because all the commands of God are meant to give us joy, not rob us of it.

To Whom Do I Confess?

Please, do not think we should be running around telling every person about our sins. The purpose of us confessing our sins is for healing; therefore, we need to make sure that the people we confess our sins to are the type of people who are on board with that truth. We should not be scared to ever tell our sins to anyone if we are trying to witness, or give a testimony about what God rescued us from, but constant confession should be toward specific people.

Find people in your life passionate about Jesus and living life for Him. The main people I actively confess sin to are my male friends. I am confident that when I tell them my sins, they will embrace me, lovingly rebuke me if necessary, point me to the cross, and spur me on toward repentance. I am not going to tell my sin to someone who has a loose tongue and tells everyone everything. Have you ever known a person make statements like, "Okay, you can not tell anyone this, because I promised I would not tell anyone?" That person probably does not have your best interests in mind, but rather their desire is to be exalted as a body of information.

The people I trust most are not the people who just have two ears, but who have my best interests in mind. These are people whom I have developed relationships with for a while, and I know they will not broadcast my sins. I'm certain they will be praying for me and pleading with God to give me a heart of sorrow for my own sin.

You might not have anyone in your life you can say would be that protective and reliable with the information you give him or her, and that is fine. I would then encourage you to talk to your pastor, or an elder in your church. These are people in the church who have the body's best interests in mind, and should give great advice and encouragement as you fight to see Jesus as beautiful. We can also pray that God will bring people into our lives who will become close community and lifelong friends.

Is Temptation a Sin?

We might think that every time we feel tempted, we are committing a sin. But temptation is not a sin: it is an opportunity to sin. We know this because Jesus was actually tempted and died a sinless man.

Hebrews 4:15

"For we do not have a high priest who is unable to sympathize with our weaknesses, but one who in every respect has been tempted as we are, yet without sin."

Though temptation is not a sin, I am convinced it is still something to confess. I was talking with one of my best friends the other day, and he said something that struck me: "Man, I honestly wish I had the courage to confess my temptation rather than just telling people I gave into my temptation." His comment gave me a new perspective about temptation.

There are hot lines for people who are thinking about suicide to get help before they actually commit suicide. This is the same attitude we should have with temptation. When we sin, it is a result of us giving into the temptation to believe something else is more satisfying than Jesus. If sin is deadly, why would we be silent about the temptations we have to commit deadly acts?

I believe our fight for joy as Christians would become so much more effective if we told people about the temptations we have before going to them with broken bones and all bloodied up. We should see sin as a pit and tell people we feel like jumping into it, that we believe it is going to bring satisfaction. It would be more beneficial for us to ask for help on the edge of the cliff rather than be at the bottom with broken ankles.

Satan does not want you to do this. He wants you to fight temptation on your own, and also fight sins on your own. If we move from confessing our sin to confessing our temptation, we will have more than ourselves to rely on to not sin—we will have our friend's help. It is prideful to think we do not need to tell people our desires to sin but only tell them the sins we have committed. Embrace community and confess your thoughts so that you can fight turning the thoughts into actions.

Confessing temptation has been beyond beneficial for me because I am known by my brothers and have nothing to hide. They embrace me, and help me think about Jesus as more satisfying than the promised thrill at the bottom of a pit that will surely hurt me. Everything that God commands us to do intends to lead us into Christ-likeness and satisfaction in God. Facing sins and confessing to others is a means to joy. Accountability helps us to not hide in the dark and lie about our sin, but brings us into the light to be redeemed by God.

FUEL UP

Out With the Old, In With the New

In the chapter "Shedding a Few Pounds," I was pleading with you to give up anything, whether sin or not, that gets in your way of running to God. If we are letting go of things that get in our way of being close to Christ, we are most likely going to have more time on our hands or at least be wondering if anything should replace the old. To this, I would say, yes. Letting go of things does not mean we should sit on our hands and do nothing. Instead, we should be very intentional about filling our lives with meaning and significance. We are to be joy seekers and implement things into our lives that stir our affections up for God all the more.

Have Some Fun

That's right, have fun! I am not telling you to quit your job because it is boring, or commit a crime because it is a rush and a release for you. What I am saying is "do not think that the Christian life is supposed to be void of any kind of fun." So many people, even Christians, think that Christianity is all business: serious, uptight people, no game playing, no sense of humor, and no time for any enjoyment in this life. Being around people like that is exhausting and not enjoyable. It can make you feel like you are walking on eggshells, and if any mention of fun comes from you, you will be condemned and maybe even called a hypocrite.

Of course, any of these pursuits of fun should be within the context of Scripture. When some people think "fun," they think only of serving themselves. Some people can have fun by getting really intoxicated and ignore any feelings of guilt when they have offended people in their belligerence. Some people can have fun by vandalizing property and not care about whose property they have destroyed. We must also be careful to not put a stumbling block in people's lives. In Romans 14:15-19, God warns us against making other people stumble. If we are doing something that is making a friend of ours stumble, we should be quick to avoid that action when we are in the company of that friend.

Typically, aside from the boundaries mentioned in the paragraphs above, we are free as Christians to have fun and enjoy things in life instead of always feeling bad for doing so.

Ecclesiastes 5:18-20

"Behold, what I have seen to be good and fitting is to eat and drink and find enjoyment in all the toil with which one toils under the sun the few days of his life that God has given him, for this is his lot. Everyone also to whom God has given wealth and possessions and power to enjoy them, and to accept his lot and rejoice in his toil – this is the gift of God. For he will not much remember the days of his life because God keeps him occupied with joy in his heart."

We have freedom to enjoy blessings that God gives us, and to relax in whatever ways we personally find beneficial. We are free to enjoy things in life God has blessed us with. I golf, work out, throw a football with friends, read a good book, take vacations, and learn to cook something new. How much would I enjoy those gifts God has given me and allowed me to do, if when

I was doing them all I could think was, "Oh man, I should be memorizing Scripture, praying, helping a homeless person, and learning Greek and Hebrew?" Of course, I want to make room in my life for all of these things, but if I did not think that God wanted me to enjoy those small pleasures in this life, there is no way I could find rest, rejuvenation, and relaxation in life. I would constantly be worrying about how to please Him rather than being pleased in Him by reflecting on abilities, gifts, talents, and opportunities that He has provided for me to do and enjoy more of Him in those things.

Our lives as Christians will be hard, but we should take advantage of and be thankful that God has allowed us to enjoy things in this world that bring us pleasure and give Him honor. You may work a lot, be a student with no time in the day to even think about fun, or just not know what you would like to do that is fun but not sinful. Try to carve out time, even if it is one hour a week, to do something or discover something you have fun doing. Enjoy it guilt-free, and thank God for the time you had to enjoy an activity. Do not let the world tell you that if you are a Christian you cannot have fun. That is legalism and something only people living in fear of approval do. God approves of us in the life, death, and resurrection of Jesus Christ, and He is our good father. What good father wants their kids to never have any fun?

What is it for You?

When you start to realize things in life that stir your affections for Jesus, implement more of that into your life. You might not yet know the things that stir your affections for Him, and that is okay. Ask a friend about things that they do to stir their affections up for Jesus, and try them out.

What about when I have zero time for any fun but want my heart to be happy in God? I listen to Christian Rap music, because it makes me feel hyped. The lyrics, beat, and encouragement that come from it make me want to know God more. Hanging out with friends is also important for me. Sometimes we are having fun, and sometimes we are bored out of our minds, but being around community makes me extremely happy simply because I love my friends. It allows me to rest, be thankful for friends that God gave me, and enjoy them, whether we are having fun or not. I do not know what you enjoy, but if it stirs your affections for God and does not compromise others' joy in Him, then make time for more of it, and invite some friends to tag along.

Coffee with Courtney

One of my best friends in the world is 88 years old. His name is Dick Courtney, and for about two years now, he has been my mentor. He and his wife have been missionaries for years. Everyday he goes to a few local coffee shops in hopes of meeting people, buying their coffee, and telling them about Jesus Christ. I have a lot of influences in my life, some younger and some older, but I have noticed that I cling to him often. One of my favorite things in the world is hanging out with him during the week and soaking in the wisdom he has. It has been extremely life-giving for me to have an older person I can go to for any form of advice. I find his advice to be more fool proof than the advice I could get from worldly means. Older people have much more life experience than we do and can probably shed light on challenges in our lives that are robbing us of joy.

Proverbs 20:29

"The glory of young men is their strength, but the splendor of old men is their gray hair."

Older Christians are able to instruct us in maturity, wisdom and holiness because of the long life they have experienced. I would rather take marriage advice from a couple who has been married for fifty years than a marriage counselor fresh out of their master of counseling degree who is only book smart and has no real life experience.

I highly advise you to find an older person who would be willing to meet up with you regularly and mentor you. It is a real treat from the Lord to have an older saint pour into your life. This is something you most likely are going to have to initiate. Do not assume you can go to a coffee shop and have an older person ask you to mentor you. I have learned, however, that most of our older brothers and sisters in Christ are willing, some even eager, to pour into a younger person. Do not be afraid to approach a godly older person and ask them if they would be willing to mentor you frequently. If they say no, that is fine—just seek out another person who walks with the Lord.

These meetings can take place over dinner, over a cup of coffee, or on a golf course (my favorite, as you probably already know). You do not need to be formal or dressed to the nines at your meetings to get some wisdom. Make it as casual as you want or as formal as you want, but just make time to meet up with them for an hour or two every so often. Being respectful of their time is huge. If they are going to take time to meet up with you and give you some counsel, be respectful of that, and honor your commitment by showing up on time and not cancelling.

Pick their brain. If you have a question that might seem embarrassing, do not be afraid to ask them about it. Chances are that they have experienced it firsthand, or know someone who has. Take a note pad and write down things they say that mean something to you so you do not forget them. I love quoting people who have inspired me. I encourage you to find someone older, wiser, and more mature than you are, and seek their wisdom from living this life.

Get Plugged In

By getting plugged in, I am talking about becoming a committed member to a Bible-believing, Christ-loving local church. In the chapter "Don't Fake It Till You Make It," I wrote about community and having people you confess sin to. Most of this community should be taking place with the people inside of your church. When we get involved in a local church, we love others by committing to serve them.

I know so many people in college who have and are currently church-hopping. This means that they are involved a little bit here and a little bit there in different churches. They are committed to this church's weekly event, and that church's worship service. They are not able to fully commit to a group of people, because they do not dig roots anywhere. They only spread a little bit of themselves all over the church community.

Laying down roots in one church allows us to go deeper with people. This does not mean your church is the best or even the healthiest church around, but it does mean you are reliable to your church. If they need you for something, you are not busy with another church's event. This helps us to understand commitment on a whole new level. When something else seems flashy or more thrilling, we turn it down because of our commitment to one. As a husband *should* be committed to one wife, he is to be engaged in and committed to *his* wife *alone*. Being fully committed to my local church has been life-giving for me—going to church member meetings, plugging in to weekly Bible studies, serving with communion and offering, helping clean up if needed, and volunteering for events.

Some of you might read this portion and think, "Yeah, no thanks; I'm not accepted in the church because of X, Y, and Z." Maybe the church has burned you, and you are okay with just being a Christian on your own. My question to you would be, how can you proclaim to be a Bible-believing, Jesus-seeking person, and think that living this life alone, with no community and no one to confess sin to, is okay? It is not! Do not let the imperfectly executed love of God from any of His people drive you away from obedience and commitment to a local church body. The church we need to be avoiding is the one that proclaims to have it all together, the one where everyone is happy, chipper, and has no problems and no mess. Let me know when you find one of those this side of glory. The kind of church we should be committed to is one where there are real people with real brokenness and real problems trying to trust in God with it all, and who are honest about their state. No church is going to be able to grow if their problems are kept quiet.

In a short article called "The Religious Life of Theological Students," Benjamin B. Warfield writes this:

"No man can withdraw himself from the stated religious services of the community of which he is a member, without serious injury to his personal religious life."[10]

It is dangerous to your own soul to withdraw from or to not engage in a community of Bible-believing people. Friends, for your own joy, plug in to a local church that loves Jesus and takes the Bible seriously. If you are already attending a local church, find ways to serve rather than to just sit in the service on Sunday mornings. It is for your own good and for the good of others!

God desires for us to know Him and His love for broken sinners. Incredibly, He leads us to other people to join us in the fight for our joy in Him. Have some fun, find a mentor, get plugged into a local church, and invite people into your life as a whole, not just in part. God intends to use others to help us see Him as more beautiful and more satisfying than anything in this world.

---

10. Benjamin B. Warfield, "The Religious Life of Theological Students," accessed July 21, 2016, https://www.tms.edu/m/tmsj6g.pdf.

CONCLUSION

Nothing we can ever do will help us gain the favor of God. The bar is set too high for us to ever reach. We have all been crippled by sin and we are always leaving a trail that highlights the fact that we have, once again, fallen short of the glory of God. Because of this truth, we might ask the questions, "Why obey? Why should I put forth effort, if even on my best day, it will not be enough?"

Paul Tripp explains the answers to these questions exceptionally well in a recent post of his called "Why Obedience?" Here is how he explains why we should obey even though obedience is not enough to earn God's favor.

So what's the point of obedience in the Christian life? Well, this hard-to-swallow pill of bad news is actually the doorway to eternal hope and joy, not depressive self-loathing. How? It's only when you accept who you are and what you're unable to do that you begin to understand and celebrate the necessity of God's gift of grace.

Let's put the bad news and the good news together. The Apostle Paul writes, "for all have sinned and fall short of the glory of God," but that's only half of the story. He continues, "and are justified by his grace as a gift, through the redemption that is in Christ Jesus, whom God put forward as a propitiation by his blood, to be received by faith" (Romans 3:23-25).

Propitiation is an atoning sacrifice. The sacrifice of Jesus appeased the wrath of God and created reconciliation between God and all who place their faith in Him. In more simple words: you do not need to obey to gain God's favor.

Do not misunderstand me; grace does not make obedience optional. Obedience is the life-long calling for followers of Christ, but your obedience is never a fearful payment. It is a hymn of gratitude to the God who met you where you were, and did for you what you could not have done for yourself. Your obedience does not purchase God's love for you. Christ's blood is the only purchase that could do that. Rather, your obedience is a thankful expression, that you understand the significance of God's love being placed on you. So today, humbly admit that you are more messed up than you think you are, and commit once more to a lifestyle of obedience, not because Jesus needs you to, but because you understand how much you need Jesus.[11]

Tripp shines light on a simple but breathtaking truth in his response to why we should obey. Jesus does not need us to obey Him, but because we need Jesus desperately, and because He gave himself up for us, obedience then is the response to the reality, that Christ laid down His life for ours when we were at our worst (Romans 5:8). Gratitude should lead us to obedience, and obedience to Joy.

Friends, my plea for you is to "Choose Joy." Let your heart daily be reminded of the amazing love of God. Be amazed that Jesus Christ obeyed the Father's will to take on your unrighteousness and to give you His righteousness. Be thankful God is totally satisfied in His son Jesus Christ, and that Jesus Christ is our representative in the court of God. Then walk in

---

11. Paul Tripp, "Why Obedience?" accessed July 21, 2016, http://www.paultripp.com/ wednesdays-word/posts/why-obedience.

obedience, not begrudgingly, but joyfully as an expression of a heart that desires to experience more of God every day.

John 15:9-11

As the Father has loved me, so have I loved you. Abide in my love. If you keep my commandments, you will abide in my love, just as I have kept my Father's commandments and abide in his love. These things I have spoken to you, that my joy may be in you, and that your joy may be full.